D0118724

PERSPECTIVES ON THE
GREAT DEPRESSION

by Linden K. McNeilly

12 STORY LIBRARY

www.12StoryLibrary.com

12-Story Library is an imprint of Bookstaves and Press Room Editions

Produced for 12-Story Library by Red Line Editorial

Photographs ©: AP Images, cover, 1, 7, 12, 14, 16, 17, 19, 28; Everett Historical/Shutterstock Images, 4, 5, 8, 9, 10, 11, 13, 20, 21, 23, 24, 25; Gordon Parks/Farm Security Administration/Office of War Information Black-and-White Negatives/Library of Congress, 18; Alan Fisher/New York World-Telegram and the Sun Newspaper Photograph Collection/Library of Congress, 26; Brown Brothers/Library of Congress, 27; Courtesy Everett Collection/Rex Features/AP Images, 29

Content Consultant: Jason E. Taylor, Professor, Department of Economics, Central Michigan University

Library of Congress Cataloging-in-Publication Data
978-1-63235-401-3 (hardcover)
978-1-63235-473-0 (paperback)
978-1-62143-525-9 (ebook)

Printed in the United States of America
022017

Access free, up-to-date content on this topic plus a full digital version of this book. Scan the QR code on page 31 or use your school's login at 12StoryLibrary.com.

Table of Contents

Fact Sheet 4

Banking Crisis Causes Big Problems 6

Families Have to Make Sacrifices 8

Veterans Demand What They Were Promised 10

Herbert Hoover Takes the Blame 12

A New President Offers a New Deal 14

Women Are Off to Work 16

Black Americans Get a Raw Deal 18

Sharecroppers Work to Get Ahead 20

More Students Stay in School 22

Farmers Can't Sell Any Crops 24

Young People Ride the Rails 26

Americans Use Entertainment to Forget Their Troubles 28

Glossary 30

For More Information 31

Index 32

About the Author 32

Fact Sheet

What was the Great Depression?

The Great Depression was the worst economic time in US history. It started in 1929 and lasted until 1939.

How did the Great Depression happen?

The Great Depression started with the stock market collapse on October 29, 1929. The stock market allows companies to raise money by selling part of their ownership, or shares. People who bought shares thought these companies would

succeed. They expected companies would pay them back. But by late 1929, stock prices were way too high. Companies could not pay back investors. Stock prices fell dramatically. This was followed by repeated banking crises that happened across the country in the early 1930s. Thousands of Americans lost their life savings.

Who was affected by the Great Depression?

Some people lost a lot of money during the stock market crash.

More importantly, however, people lost their jobs as the Depression worsened. At its height, 25 percent of Americans were out of work. Many people lost their homes and family farms.

Herbert Hoover was president from 1929 to 1933. He believed in using the federal government to help businesses. Franklin Delano Roosevelt was president from 1933 to 1945. He thought the federal government should give money directly to people in need.

Banking Crisis Causes Big Problems

After the stock market crash of 1929, many hoped the economy would recover quickly. But a banking crisis in 1930 turned the downturn in the economy into a deep depression.

In the south, a banking firm called Caldwell and Company was involved in many businesses. They provided insurance, and they loaned money for home mortgages. They had chains of smaller banks. The leader of Caldwell and Company, Rogers Caldwell, made some bad investments. His company lost a lot of money in the stock market crash. So he used most of the cash from other Caldwell and Company businesses to cover his losses. As a result, the small chain banks had smaller and smaller reserves. Without much money on hand, one of Caldwell and Company's small chain banks closed on November 7, 1930.

When news about the bank closure spread, customers at other banks panicked. They rushed to withdraw

89
Percent value stocks lost from 1929 to 1932.

- Rogers Caldwell owned a large banking firm called Caldwell and Company.
- Caldwell used money from smaller chain banks to cover his stock market losses.
- Without enough cash available, the smaller banks began to close, causing customers to lose all their savings.
- Other big banks failed, too, and the Federal Reserve did not lend money to banks to keep them open.

People mob a New York City bank in December 1930.

their money. Other banks in Caldwell and Company's chain closed. This started a domino effect. Some people woke up to find all their savings gone.

Other big banks around the country failed, too. The banking branch of the US government is called the Federal Reserve. It is supposed to help banks when they run out of reserves by loaning them money. But the Federal Reserve did not do its job during the Great Depression. It allowed these big banks to fail.

Families Have to Make Sacrifices

For many families, life became much harder during the Great Depression. In some middle-income families, only the fathers worked outside the home. When those fathers lost their jobs, many people went hungry. At the Great Depression's worst point in 1933, one out of four workers were unemployed.

Many others had hours and wages cut. The average family income was $2,300 per year in 1929. That figure dropped to $1,500 by 1933.

Many people believed at the time that it was the father's responsibility to provide for his family. When fathers could not find work, they

Soup kitchen in Washington, DC

15 million

Number of people who were unemployed in 1933 because of the Great Depression.

- Families' incomes dropped by almost 35 percent over four years.
- Some went without basic items, such as toothpaste and toilet paper.
- People stopped throwing things away and repurposed them instead.

took the news hard. And even though prices dropped, many things were still too expensive to afford. Families learned to do without basic items, such as toothpaste. They used baking soda instead. For toilet paper, they used newspapers or magazine pages. Churches and other religious organizations arranged soup and bread lines in large cities. They provided food to those who couldn't afford it.

Women learned to stretch food by adding inexpensive ingredients, such as potatoes and noodles. Every household item could be saved and

Stores lowered their prices to try to get customers to buy their products.

repurposed. Shoes were stuffed with cardboard when the soles wore out. Worn-out sheets were cut and resewn with other sheets. Towels were mended or cut down and made into washcloths. Many people never stopped saving things, even when times got better.

THINK ABOUT IT

During the Great Depression, a tube of toothpaste cost 25¢, and a small radio cost $40. Many families saved in order to purchase a radio but couldn't afford toothpaste. Why would families choose an expensive radio over toothpaste?

DEPRESSION ERA SHOPPING

Shop owners lowered their prices to try to sell things. In 1933, milk was just 9¢ per quart. Bread was 6¢. And a new white shirt was only $1.95. But even at very low prices, some things were just too expensive for some families.

3
Veterans Demand What They Were Promised

In 1932, many Americans were struggling. World War I (1914–1918) veterans were no different. In May of that year, one veteran named Walter Waters led a group of a few hundred unemployed veterans to Washington, DC. Thousands more joined them. The group became known as the Bonus Marchers. In 1924, the government promised to pay the WWI veterans a bonus.

The bonus was supposed to be paid in 1945, but the veterans argued they needed the money right away. They camped out in Washington, DC, and set up shanties made of wood or cardboard. They were determined to stay until the bonus was paid.

In June 1932, Congress introduced a bill to pay the veterans. When the House of Representatives passed the bill, the veterans were optimistic. But President Herbert Hoover

Bonus Marchers stood on the steps of the Senate building in the summer of 1932.

Veterans and police officers clashed on July 28, 1932.

promised to veto the bill. He claimed the government did not have enough money to pay the bonuses early. Then the Senate failed to pass the bill. The veterans stayed.

In late July, President Hoover ordered the US Army to remove the veterans. General Douglas MacArthur and his soldiers used machine guns, tanks, and tear gas to make the veterans leave. They set fire to the shanties. Some veterans were injured. The public and many other politicians were shocked at how the veterans were treated. The veterans returned home without their bonuses.

20,000
Estimated number of veterans who joined the Bonus March.

- Unemployed veterans wanted the government to pay them a bonus in advance.
- The Bonus Marchers promised to stay in Washington, DC, until the bonus was paid.
- The Senate did not agree to pay the bonus early.
- President Hoover ordered General MacArthur and the US Army to get rid of the marchers.

Herbert Hoover Takes the Blame

Herbert Hoover became an orphan at age 9 and started working when he was just 14 years old. He went to college at Stanford University and eventually became a mining engineer and a millionaire. In 1928, he won the presidential election in a landslide.

The stock market crashed just eight months after he took office. Hoover was sympathetic to people who lost their jobs. Before becoming president, he helped many people who were starving in Europe during World War I. But Hoover was certain that using the federal government to give money directly to the unemployed was wrong. He thought help should come from neighbors, churches, and other local groups.

He tried using the government to create jobs with public works projects. His plan didn't work. More people lost their jobs, and the unemployment rate rose. In 1931, 7 million people were looking for work. By 1933, that number had increased to 15 million.

President Hoover signs a relief bill in 1930.

1919

Year Herbert Hoover established the Hoover Institution, a research center at Stanford.

- Hoover overcame challenges early in his life.
- The stock market crashed eight months after he took office.
- He refused to use the federal government to directly aid the unemployed and tried to create jobs instead.
- His plan failed, and many Americans blamed him for not fixing the economic problems.

Hooverville in Manhattan, New York, 1932

Many Americans felt he could have done more. People who had lost their homes started living on the edges of towns. They used boxes, empty railroad cars, or sewer pipes for shelter. The public called these slums Hoovervilles. Many blamed the president for not helping Americans get back on their feet. Although he ran again for president in 1932, Hoover was not surprised when Franklin Delano Roosevelt was elected instead.

HOOVER BLANKETS

Hoover became so hated that people started attaching his name to evidence of their troubles. "Hoover blankets" were old newspapers used for warmth. Empty pockets turned inside out were called "Hoover flags." When people caught jackrabbits for food, they were called "Hoover hogs." And "Hoover wagons" were broken-down cars pulled by mules.

A New President Offers a New Deal

In 1932, the nation looked for someone other than President Hoover to help fix the country. Franklin Delano Roosevelt, or FDR, was elected as the next president in a landslide victory during that year. FDR was the first president to speak directly to the public. He talked to Americans during his fireside chats on the radio. He promised them the government would take action and help them recover.

FDR believed the Great Depression could be stopped only if the federal government got involved. Unlike Hoover, FDR thought it was his duty to get directly involved. He called his federal programs

the New Deal. Together with Congress, he passed the Social Security Act. This program uses funds from the federal government to give money to people who are

FDR
in 1933

500,000

Number of people who wrote to FDR in his first week in office.

- FDR was elected in a landslide in 1932.
- He believed it was the government's duty to help people.
- FDR created a series of programs called the New Deal, and some are still around today.
- Some of FDR's government programs made things worse.

unable to work. Some of these people include those who are old and retired and people with disabilities. Social Security is still around today. So is federal bank insurance and unemployment insurance, which were both passed under FDR.

One of FDR's most successful programs was called the Civilian Conservation Corps (CCC). Another was the Works Progress Administration (WPA). Together, these two programs hired 8 million men who couldn't find work elsewhere. They dug ditches, built roads, planted trees, and built parks. FDR knew that work would give the men purpose and reduce unemployment. He hoped the nation would become more optimistic.

The government under FDR tried many new things. While some changes made life better for Americans, some made things worse. His government encouraged farmers to reduce the amount of food for sale so prices would rise. This meant some food went to waste at a time when some Americans were starving. Nevertheless, FDR is considered one of the greatest presidents of the 1900s.

Women Are Off to Work

Women have faced inequality in the workforce for a long time. The pressures of the Great Depression meant women experienced prejudice during this time, too. Women who wanted jobs were sometimes pressured to stay away from higher paying ones. Many thought men should have those jobs to provide for their families. The CCC had a formal policy against hiring women. Even women's colleges asked their students not to pursue careers after graduation so those jobs could be filled by men. One journalist suggested firing all the women in the country as a way to solve the unemployment rate for men.

But women's rates of employment actually went up slightly during the Depression. Clerical workers, housekeepers, teachers, nurses, and telephone operators found work. These were jobs that men were not likely to take. Sometimes women were the only breadwinners in

Women working as telephone operators in 1933

their families. They had no choice but to work.

Eleanor Roosevelt was America's First Lady from 1933 through 1945. She was very influential. Eleanor traveled around the country. She saw firsthand how hard life was for many Americans. She reported back to FDR about what she witnessed. She championed the rights of black people, women, and children. Eleanor was determined to help them. She used her newspaper column "My Day" to speak directly to the public, providing reassurance and hope. She received thousands of letters and sent many small personal checks to help individuals stay afloat.

10.5 million
Women who worked outside the home in 1930.

- The public often pressured women to keep them from taking jobs away from men.
- Women's employment actually went up during the Great Depression.
- Women were sometimes the only breadwinners in their families.
- First Lady Eleanor Roosevelt supported women's causes and often sent money to the people who wrote to her.

Eleanor Roosevelt speaks out about women's rights during a 1939 radio broadcast.

Black Americans Get a Raw Deal

The Great Depression affected black people much more harshly than it did white people. Employers laid off black people first. Entry-level jobs traditionally held by black people, such as housekeeping, were taken by white people now desperate for work. Even when the federal government offered aid, black people could face prejudice. Under FDR's New Deal, public housing was separated by race. Some black people did find jobs with the CCC and the WPA. But they often faced discrimination from their supervisors.

Mary McLeod Bethune founded the National Youth Administration.

50
Percentage of black people who were unemployed in 1930.

- Black people were hit much harder than white people by the Great Depression.
- They were discriminated against by employers and the general public.
- Black people helped one another to raise rent.
- Some black leaders worked with FDR to help improve the lives of black people.

First Lady Eleanor Roosevelt presents Marion Anderson with an award in 1939.

Some businesses hired mainly white people when most of their customers were black. Black people pushed back. "Don't buy where you don't work" became a motto in Chicago and other cities in 1929. Black people also banded together with friends to hold rent parties. These events helped raise money for rent by having ticketed dance parties.

When Eleanor Roosevelt began speaking out about racial inequality, FDR started to listen. Civil rights activist Mary McLeod Bethune became one of FDR's top advisers. She worked with FDR to help young black people get an education and find work.

DISCRIMINATION AT THE OPERA

Marion Anderson was a famous black opera singer. She had hoped to sing at Constitution Hall in Washington, DC, in 1939. But the Daughters of the American Revolution (DAR), the organization that owned the building, did not allow it. Eleanor Roosevelt was a member of the DAR and resigned in protest. She organized a concert at the Lincoln Memorial, with approximately 75,000 attendees. Anderson later appeared at Constitution Hall for various concerts, after the DAR developed a more inclusive policy.

Sharecroppers Work to Get Ahead

Sharecroppers lived and worked on farms, but they didn't own the land. They did the work of planting, fertilizing, and harvesting crops. Sharecroppers paid landowners a portion of the crops they grew.

The landowners took as much as half of the crops grown. The sharecroppers got housing and tools to use in return. Many sharecroppers were black. In the South, less than 20 percent of black people owned land. But they represented 40 percent of those farm workers.

Sharecroppers' lives were dependent on the honesty of the landowners. Sharecroppers often had to borrow

$100 million

Amount the US government paid to help farmers in 1933.

- Sharecroppers worked and lived on farms and sometimes had to take out loans to buy food and clothes.
- Government aid was supposed to help sharecroppers, but some landowners kept all the money for themselves.
- Some sharecroppers protested while others moved north in the hope of better treatment.

A sharecropper sorts tobacco in 1938.

Evicted sharecroppers protest in Georgia in 1939.

money from landowners to buy food and clothes until harvest time. Unfortunately, some landowners charged high interest rates on those loans. Most were also very aware of the fact that many sharecroppers could not read or write. Some landowners knowingly cheated sharecroppers out of profits.

In 1933 under FDR, the government provided aid to landowners. To raise food prices, the government paid them to not grow crops. Part of that money was supposed to go to sharecroppers if they rented the land. Many landowners realized if they evicted the sharecroppers, they could keep all the money for themselves. Some evicted sharecroppers protested and formed unions. Many moved to northern states in search of better options.

SOCIAL SECURITY ACT

The Social Security Act of 1935 is one of FDR's most well-known programs from the New Deal. Social Security was meant to provide retired workers with a source of income. But Social Security did not cover all workers when it was first introduced. People who worked on farms were specifically excluded from receiving Social Security. Combined with other exclusions, more than 65 percent of black people were not eligible for Social Security in 1935.

More Students Stay in School

In the 1920s, people began to focus on education. Teachers received higher salaries than ever before. Communities built new schools. Things changed after 1932. Some towns and cities could not pay back loans they had taken out to build new schools. Bankers wanted to cut teachers' salaries in response. Many teachers continued to work for less pay because having a job was better than being unemployed. Schools in Dayton, Ohio, were open three days a week to save money.

Since it was hard to find jobs, more students went to school during the Great Depression. In 1930, an estimated 4.4 million teens went to high school. By 1940, this number grew to 6.5 million. More students

CHILDREN AT WORK

Jobs were hard to find during the Great Depression. In spite of this, a few children were still able to find part-time work to help support their families. Most of these jobs went to boys. Some delivered newspapers. Others worked as store clerks.

70
Percentage of new schools constructed from 1933 to 1939 that were built by the PWA.

- Teachers' salaries were cut.
- More teens went to high school since it was hard to find jobs.
- Classroom sizes grew when more students stayed in school.
- The PWA built thousands of new schools during the Great Depression.

A teacher passes out grapefruits from the Red Cross.

received high school diplomas than ever before.

Schools were not always prepared to take on the growing number of students. Classroom sizes grew. Students also had to share textbooks more often. In some cases, students had to share one textbook with the entire class.

The nation needed more schools. Between 1933 and 1939, the Public Works Administration (PWA) built thousands of new schools. The PWA was part of FDR's New Deal.

Farmers Can't Sell Any Crops

Being a farmer during the Great Depression was very difficult. As long as people had money to spend, farmers could make a living. But everything changed after the Great Depression struck. With so many unemployed, people couldn't afford to buy wheat, corn, and cotton. Demand fell enormously.

Low demand led to too much crop. This surplus drove prices down. Some farmers took drastic measures to improve demand. Wisconsin farmers hijacked milk trucks and spilled their contents in an effort to raise milk prices. Unfortunately, it didn't help in the long run.

Though families worked hard to keep their farms, about a third were in too much debt. Then banks tried to take the farms and sell them. Sometimes

This family farm was sold at auction in 1938.

THIS·135 ACRE/ FARM Will Be Sold at· PUBLIC·AUCTION ON·PREMISES JULY 30 1·P·M. Dr M.C.MOSES.Owner, New Carlisle Ohio,

Programs from the New Deal encouraged farmers to use fertilizers.

STARVED BY LACK OF PLANT FOOD

NOURISHED ON PHOSPHATE AND LIME

30
Approximate percentage of Americans who lived on farms in 1934.

- Farmers grew lots of crops, but not enough people bought them.
- Prices fell when there was a surplus of crops.
- Banks took away farms when farmers had too much debt.
- President Hoover and President Roosevelt tried to help farmers, but the aid often came too late.

fellow farmers banded together to prevent them from being auctioned.

President Hoover offered government loans to farmers. He did not think the government should offer farmers money they would not have to pay back. Farmers did receive free aid under FDR. But it wasn't easy to fix farming problems. Despite new laws protecting land and farmers, help came too late for many farming families.

Young People Ride the Rails

In the 1930s, many left their homes to search for something better. Some who left were children and teens. They typically had younger siblings and believed they were helping their families. Leaving meant there was one less mouth to feed.

Young people rode the rails looking for opportunity and adventure. Some rode trains to wherever they could find farm work. They would harvest corn and wheat in the Midwest, hay in California, and fruits in the Pacific Northwest. Many young people had never left their hometowns before.

A young man hops aboard a train in 1935.

250,000
Estimated number of teenagers riding the rails at the height of the Great Depression.

- Many young people left their homes so there would be one less mouth to feed.
- Catching trains allowed some to find work and travel to new places.
- Riding the rails was dangerous and illegal.
- Thousands of people died trying to jump on or off moving trains.

A railroad worker on top chases away a rail rider.

Jumping on moving trains and traveling great distances was exciting. The trick was not to get injured or caught.

Riding the rails meant jumping into open boxcars or grabbing the ladder between the cars as the train was moving. It was dangerous and illegal. Teenagers riding the rails also had to worry about being caught by train guards, called bulls. Bulls would force people off the trains, sometimes at gunpoint. Bulls would also take whatever money the riders had on them as payment for taking the train illegally.

Americans Use Entertainment to Forget Their Troubles

During the Great Depression, many Americans wanted to forget about their troubles for a while. They often turned to the main source of home entertainment: the radio. Families gathered around it to listen to shows with drama, romance, music, and comedy.

Americans also saved their coins to buy a ticket to the movies. Movie theaters needed the business, so many reduced ticket prices. Movies offered people a way to escape the hardships of the real world for a few hours. Walt Disney released its first animated feature-length cartoon, *Snow White and the Seven Dwarfs*, in 1937. Many didn't

A crowd waits to see *Gone with the Wind* in New York.

THINK ABOUT IT

Why was entertainment so important during the Great Depression? What does this say about people's needs beyond food and shelter? What role does entertainment serve today, and is it different from then?

The Wizard of Oz was nominated for Best Picture at the Academy Awards in 1940.

think the public would like sitting through an 80-minute-long fairy tale. But audiences were wild about it. It became so popular it broke attendance records at the time.

Just two years later, *The Wizard of Oz* came out in 1939. It used Technicolor to shift from black-and-white scenes set in Kansas to show the colorful fairyland of Oz. The movie was especially popular with children.

10¢
Price of a child's movie ticket during the Great Depression.

- Americans escaped their harsh lives through entertainment.
- Many radio shows provided daily entertainment.
- People went to the movies to escape reality for a few hours.
- *Snow White and the Seven Dwarfs* broke attendance records.

29

Glossary

breadwinner
The person in a family or household who is mainly responsible for earning money to support the others.

evict
To force someone to move from a home or a piece of land.

evidence
Factual information that helps prove whether something is true or not true.

insurance
A policy of paying money to a person or company faced with unfortunate events.

landslide
A large majority of votes in an election.

optimistic
Believing that things will turn out for the best.

prejudice
A fixed or unfair opinion about someone based on their race or gender.

shanties
Small shelters that are not sturdy.

slum
An area of a town or city where poor people live in crowded and run-down conditions.

surplus
An amount greater than needed.

unemployed
When a person does not have a job or work.

veterans
People who have fought in a war or conflict.

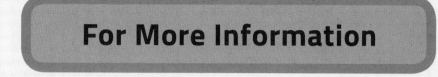

For More Information

Books

Mullenbach, Cheryl. *The Great Depression for Kids*. Chicago: Chicago Review Press, 2015.

Nardo, Don. *The Presidency of Franklin D. Roosevelt: Confronting the Great Depression and World War II*. North Mankato, MN: Compass Point Books, 2015.

Pascal, Janet. *What Was the Great Depression?* New York: Grosset & Dunlap, 2015.

Visit 12StoryLibrary.com

Scan the code or use your school's login at **12StoryLibrary.com** for recent updates about this topic and a full digital version of this book. Enjoy free access to:

- Digital ebook
- Breaking news updates
- Live content feeds
- Videos, interactive maps, and graphics
- Additional web resources

Note to educators: Visit 12StoryLibrary.com/register to sign up for free premium website access. Enjoy live content plus a full digital version of every 12-Story Library book you own for every student at your school.

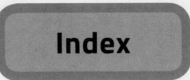

Index

Anderson, Marion, 19

banking crisis, 6–7
Bonus Marchers, 10

Caldwell and Company, 6–7
Caldwell, Rogers, 6
Civilian Conservation Corps (CCC), 15, 16, 18
crops, 20–21, 24

discrimination, 16–17, 18–19

entertainment, 28–29

family life, 8–9, 26
farmers, 15, 24–25
Federal Reserve, 7
fireside chats, 14

Hoover, Herbert, 10, 11, 12–13, 14, 25
Hoovervilles, 13

MacArthur, Douglas, 11
McLeod Bethune, Mary, 19

New Deal, 14–15, 18, 21

Roosevelt, Eleanor, 17, 19
Roosevelt, Franklin Delano (FDR), 13, 14–15, 17, 18, 19, 21, 25

school, 22–23
sharecroppers, 20–21
Social Security Act, 14–15, 21
soup kitchens, 9

teenagers, 22, 26–27
trains, 26–27

veterans, 10–11

Works Progress Administration (WPA), 15, 18

About the Author

Linden K. McNeilly taught public school for many years. She now writes children's books and lives in California with her family.